Explaining

"Teaching Machines"

and

Programming

By DAVID CRAM

Division of Audio-visual Services
San Jose State College

Fearon Publishers
San Francisco

Objectives

When you have finished reading this book, you should be able to define the term "teaching machine," and distinguish between devices that fit the definition and those that don't. You should be able to describe the relationship between the machine and its program with some understanding of the relative importance of each. You will have had practice in working through two styles of programming and will have an acquaintance with some of the rationale and advantages of these two styles. You will have read about two other programming styles and, finally, will have been introduced to some advantages, actual and potential, of the machines themselves.

Foreword

This afternoon, a school principal asked me, "What would be your advice to us about 'teaching machines'? We are being visited by salesmen, and we think there must be something we should do to be prepared to analyze the whole teaching machine idea." I wish that this book had been in my hand to give to him! It is my belief that he, and others concerned with education, would be helped by it.

Are you one of these: a teacher, a future teacher, a teacher of teachers, a school administrator, a school board member, a parent, a citizen concerned with the welfare and future of education? If you are, it is my guess that you will enjoy this book, and will find it will take you on your first step toward understanding programs and teaching machines. This is all to the good, too, since it seems inevitable that what are now known as "teaching machines" and "programmed self-instruction" will hold a significant place in educational programs in the immediate future.

That wise decisions be made in the selection and use of programs is of great importance; that the values and special contributions of teaching machines be understood by all concerned is an urgent necessity.

Before adopting programmed instruction and teaching machines, the judicious will, of course, ask many questions and deserve clear answers: How do teaching machines and programs fit into the pattern of traditional instruction? What do they replace? What do they supplement? Will teaching machines help teachers to be more effective, and if so, in what ways? What can programs and machines contribute to the solution of immediate and continuing problems of education? Will students using programs learn more, learn better, learn faster than by present procedures? In what subjects and in which grade levels can programmed self-instruction be used? And, simply, and *first*, what *is* programmed self-instruction, and what *are* teaching machines?

For people asking questions such as these, I believe this book is a practical and useful introduction. Not that it tells all that is known or all that is needed to be known! But it does explain and illustrate this new and challenging technique in education.

RICHARD B. LEWIS
San Jose State College
June 1961

Contents:

Introducing the
Scrambled Book

No matter whether you have heard only distant rumblings about "teaching machines" or whether you belong to the swelling legion who are all fired up about them, sooner or later you will wonder what kind you or your school district should buy. Well please don't buy yet — let this book give you some background first.

This book is programmed like a "teaching machine" — some call it a "scrambled" book. If you are familiar with this type of book, there's no need for you to read the explanation that follows — just turn to page 8 and plunge right in.

□ □ □ □ □

The purpose of this book is, in part, to explain programming. Since this is in itself a programmed book, I won't give you, at this point, a detailed discussion of the reason for its structure. Instead, I'll tell you what to expect, and a little of why, and ask your patience in following it through to the fuller explanations that come later.

A "scrambled" book first presents an amount of information, usually less than one page. The reader must then make a response to indicate whether or not he understands the information presented. The response he makes directs him to the next page he is to read in the program. The new page will either correct misconceptions or present new information. The pages are numbered consecutively, but the content is scrambled to prevent anticipating where the correct answer page may be found; this compels attention. Now it is time to begin the program. PLEASE TURN TO PAGE 8. AND REMEMBER, YOU CAN'T READ THE PAGES IN SEQUENCE.

NOTE: If you came to this page from page one, you came the wrong way. The pages in this book can't be read in sequence, so please go back to page one and read the directions.

While it is certainly possible to require responses from students during a motion picture showing, either through a film especially designed for this purpose or by interrupting the showing at certain moments, these response requirements are directed indifferently at all students. The slowest student in the audience is required to answer at the same rate as the fastest student — and one of advantages of "teaching machines" is that this lock-step is, if not finally broken, at least being seriously challenged.

Please reread the question on page 4 and choose the other alternative.

Right! While we are possibly coming closer to a "teaching machine," a class is not an individual; and the "teaching machine" is designed so that the student can work *individually* with a measure of control over his own rate of progress.

To qualify as a "teaching machine," a motion picture would have to:

1. First present information and then ask for periodic responses from the student.
2. Shut itself off and wait for the student to make his response and then start the projector again.
3. Inform the student, after he had restarted the projector, of the appropriateness of his response.

Dr. A. A. Lumsdaine designed a machine in which films contained in pre-threaded magazines are inserted into a projector and projected onto a small screen. In one application, a how-to-do-it film was used to show a technician how to repair a device he had never seen before. After each step in the procedure was shown, the projector stopped while the technician imitated what he had seen. When each step was completed, the technician restarted the machine and went on to the next step.

Does this now constitute a "teaching machine"?
    Page 5   Yes
    Page 10   No

Right! The educational motion picture, as it is normally used, is not a "teaching machine."

1. Although the motion picture presents information, it does not require periodic responses from the student in the form of answers, selections, or motor responses.
2. Since it does not ask for responses, it does not indicate whether the responses are appropriate or not.
3. It does not allow the individual class member to adjust his rate of progress to his own needs and capabilities.

Imagine, however, an educational motion picture which requires that the students answer questions periodically on a printed answer form. Would this then constitute a "teaching machine"?

Page 2   Yes
Page 12   No

Suppose an inattentive or unqualified person were to try to repair the device, using this machine to help. One mistake on the part of the technician could be disastrous. There is no way to guarantee that a mistake will be noticed, because no means are provided for either the machine or the student to detect erroneous responses. If a mistake is made, it will be noticed only by chance.

Please return to page 3 and take the other alternative.

The educational motion picture, as it is normally used, *does* present factual information but does *not* satisfy any of the other conditions set down for a "teaching machine;" no response is called for, no feedback is given, and the student has no control over his rate of progress.

The standard educational motion picture, then, is similar to a well-prepared lecture, but is not a "teaching machine."

Please read the conditions on page 8 again and then select the other alternative.

At last we've set up the conditions under which a motion picture and a projector can constitute a "teaching machine." Notice that it is the *organization (programming) of the film and the way it is used,* and not the projector, that determines whether it is a "teaching machine."

What, then, is meant by the term "teaching machine"? This term has been used loosely to refer to programmed self-instruction in general; but as we have seen, the organization of the program (and the program itself) determine whether it fits the criteria. We could, perhaps, refer to the machine simply as a "program holder" thus placing it in a more appropriate relationship to the program; but while this would be adequate for most of the machines now in existence, it would exclude machines that add important instructional dimensions of their own. In this book, for want of better terminology, "program" will refer to content and organization; "machine" will mean most presentation devices; and "program holder" will include programmed books (like this one) and the simplest of machines.

Please accept a word of caution: In the field of programmed self-instruction, the newcomer is often confronted with flashing lights, levers, and other intricate and exciting visual and auditory events, making it too easy to be dazzled by the presentation device before the essence of the matter — the program — is even mentioned. Since the same "program" may often be adaptable to several different modes of presentation, only some of which require machines, I shall deliberately play down the role of the machine until later, when we'll see that there may be distinct advantages to machines in some situations.

Please choose between these statements:

Page 14 I accept your remarks about programs and machines, at least for the time being.

Page 13 I'm not sure I understand what's so wrong with getting the machines first and **then** figuring out the best ways of using them.

Definition of the Term
"Teaching Machine"

In 1924, Dr. Sidney L. Pressey invented a small machine that would score a multiple-choice examination automatically at the time the answer-button was pushed.

Although he designed it as a testing machine, he perceived that by a simple expedient he could use the machine as a teaching device. All he had to do was to design it so that, for each question, the correct answer-button had to be pushed before a subsequent question would appear in the window.

From this simple beginning, the concept of "teaching machines" has grown until now the educator is faced with many types and styles, from the simplest cardboard device costing pennies to incredibly complex electronic wonders costing thousands of dollars.

But don't despair. All "teaching machines" have three characteristics in common:

1. They present information and require frequent responses by the student.
2. They provide immediate feedback to the student, informing him whether his response is appropriate or not.
3. They allow the student to work individually and to adjust his own rate of progress to his own needs and capabilities.

Now, based on the three criteria listed above, is the educational motion picture, as it is normally used, a "teaching machine"?

Page 6   Yes

Page 4   No

A class is not an individual. There is no guarantee that at the end of the discussion everyone in the class will have participated, or even that more than a few ever understand the argument.

This is not to say that this wouldn't be a very useful teaching method — it can be — but it isn't a "teaching machine."

Please return to page 12 and select the other alternative.

Your answer is correct. The first condition (providing information and requiring a response) is met; and so is the third (the student works individually and adjusts his own rate of progress); but, as you perceived, the student is not specifically directed to evaluate his response against the correct response. The success of the whole operation hinges on the clarity of the film and the student's ability to relate what he does to what he has seen.

In this case, however, the device *could* be a "teaching machine" *except for the way the film is organized.*

Suppose the film, inserted in Lumsdaine's machine, were to go through sequences like this one:

1. A short discussion is presented on techniques of violin bowing.
2. A particular technique is then demonstrated, and the narrator asks the student to identify the technique.
3. The projector shuts itself off.
4. The student (after he has made his response) pushes a button to start the projector again, and the narrator identifies the appropriate answer, giving the reason.
5. The film then proceeds to the next step in the lesson.

Would this constitute a "teaching machine"?
Page 7   Yes
Page 11   No

This time we really have a teaching machine!

All the requirements are here:
1. The film presents information and requests a response (identify the bowing technique).
2. The projector stops, waiting to be restarted by the student after his response is made.
3. The film, when restarted, identifies the appropriate answer.

The student goes at his own pace, since it is he who starts the projector after each response is made.

Please return to page 10 and select the other alternative.

Correct. A motion picture which requires that students answer questions on a printed answer form during the showing is *not* a "teaching machine."

The first condition is fulfilled since information is presented and frequent responses are required from the students.

Perhaps even feedback is provided for the student, informing him whether his response is appropriate or not.

But the third requirement, that the student be allowed to work individually and adjust his rate of progress to his own needs and capabilities, is not fulfilled since nothing is quite so inexorably paced as a movie shown to a class. The slow student — and by this I mean slow either because of mentality or lack of background or interest in a particular subject — the slow student may need time to recall previous points and ponder a bit before reaching a decision. The fast student may even anticipate the answer before the question is finished. The time interval allowed for writing the answer *must* be a compromise between the times needed for the extremes — and there we go again, playing to the "average" student!

Suppose a motion picture were designed so that during the first eight minutes an argumentative problem were set up followed by the instruction to turn off the projector and hold a class discussion with a promise of a solution in the last two minutes of the film. Would this qualify as a "teaching machine"?

Page 9   Yes
Page 3   No

You don't see what's wrong with getting the machines first and then figuring out the best ways to use them? Fine. You're honest about it and I'll try to answer with an analogy.

Consider the hazards of building a program around a machine.

A Cinerama motion picture is a good example of a program made to fit a machine. You enjoy Cinerama? So do I. But consider the extent to which the content is chosen to exploit this medium.

Suppose you wanted to make a movie for Cinerama. Could you do a tender love story? A documentary on the tse-tse fly? A film on the theory of radio? Of course you *could*, but you wouldn't! The medium of Cinerama would not only be wasted on subjects like these, it would overpower them. The temptation would be to choose areas like geology or geography or the history of the loco- motive — in other words, areas that would give you lots of oppor- tunity for panoramic views of majestic subjects.

Similarly, if you buy the presentation device first, the tempta- tion will be strong to make the educational goal fit the means — the focus is too likely to be on the machine and not on the program. Please, then, accept my arguments for the present.

Turn to the self-test on page 14.

CHAPTER I — SELF-TEST

In order to summarize and review this chapter, here is a short self-test. The answers will be found on the designated page.

1. All self-instruction programs have three characteristics in common. What are these three criteria? (Use your own words. If you get stuck, look at page 8.)
2. Can a self-instruction program exist in the form of a motion picture? (page 10)
3. Does this book fit the criteria for a self-instruction program? (page 7)
4. A book can't very well be called a "machine." What term was suggested to cover the presentation of a self-instruction program in book form? (page 7)

The next question might be, "How does one go about programming?" This book does not attempt a complete answer, but it does present an introduction to some of the types of programs in current use.

Please turn the page.

Linear Programming

So far, there are two main philosophies of programming, and each results in quite a different style of program. (There is, in addition, a third group consisting of either special-purpose methods or methods which combine elements from the first two groups.)

The main styles are called:

1. Linear programs
2. Branching programs

How would you respond to this statement? There are only two possible ways of programming — linear and branching; all others are combinations of these.

Page 16   True
Page 17   False

This could be accused of being a trick question, but it was put there to remind you that we haven't yet thought up the best ways of programming. Perhaps you yourself will have that honor. We do have two major methods now, however, and we will see how each of them works.

Please return to page 15 and select the other alternative.

There is no way to know what the future developments in programming may be, but at present, *linear* and *branching* are the two most common methods used.

Having come through the first chapter of this book, you have had some experience with a branching program. So let's focus on *linear* programming for a while.

The next section of this book is in a different format from the last section. Throughout this chapter the pages are not "scrambled." The bits of information are much smaller, and much more frequent responses will be required of you. Each "frame" (information plus question) could have occupied one page by itself. Since it is not desirable to put consecutive frames on the same page (each frame includes the answer to the last frame), you must turn the page after each frame. This means that you will start reading the top frame on page 18, formulate the answer to the question, then turn to the top of page 19. There you will find the answer to the last question (on the left) and the new frame. Answer the question and continue in this fashion until you reach page 33. Following the top frame on page 33, turn back to the middle frame of page 18 and follow the same procedure with the B frames. Got it?

Turn now to page 18.

A

The first requirement of a teaching machine, remember, is that it must present information and require the student to make frequent re_____.

(Go to 19-A)

B REVIEW

responding

1. **Recall,** according to Skinner, is more efficient in the learning process than recognition.

2. The act of **responding tends to cause learning.** These two factors are the reasons for Dr. Skinner's insistence on the

_____

rather than the multiple-choice response.

(Go to 19-B)

C

constructed

Dr. Pressey's **multiple-choice** program could be visualized like this:

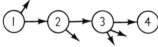

Only when the student selects the correct answer to an item will the next stimulus be presented; thus, all students follow the same sequence of multiple-choice questions. It is therefore a _____ program.

(Go to 19-C)

19

Note: this is the
answer to 18A.
Go ahead with 19A.

A

responses

Differences in belief about the <u>purpose</u> of the response have led to the development of two styles of programming. In this chapter we take up _____ programming.

(Go to 20-A)

B

constructed
response

Those two reasons for the constructed response once again:

1. _____ is more efficient than _____.

(Go to 20-B)

Ċ

linear

In a multiple-choice linear program, each student automatically ends with a correct answer, since the machines are designed so that only the correct answer-button will advance the next frame. This style of linear program was designed by Dr. P_____.

(Go to 20-C)

20

A

linear

You may have noticed that in this chapter you are no longer given a choice of pages as you were in Chapter I. <u>Everyone who reads this chapter will read the same frames in the same sequence.</u> For this reason it is a_____sequence.

(Go to 21-A)

B

recall
recognition

The second reason for the constructed response: Students may learn the wrong answers on a recognition (multiple-choice) test since the act of _____ tends to cause _____.

(End of Review)

(Go to 21-B)

C

Pressey

Pressey's defense of the multiple-choice style of linear programming is based partly on two "laws of learning." One is the **"law of frequency,"** which operates because " . . . by chance, the right response tends to be made most often since it is the only response by which the student can go to the next question." The high frequency of c_____ answers is r_____ to the student.

(Go to 21-C)

21

A

linear

Slow students—either low I.Q., low interest, or students with poor background in a subject—will perhaps read more slowly and take more time answering, but they will travel the same path as the bright student in a _____ program.

(Go to 22-A)

B

responding
learning

Another characteristic of linear programming is the **short step.** The size of each frame is large enough to handle only one short step in the total sequence. One reason is the belief that since responding tends to cause learning, the student must be allowed to make no _____.

(Go to 22-B)

C

correct
rewarding

The second "law of learning" used in defense of the multiple-choice style is the **"law of recency."** Since the correct answer is always the last one made, it is more likely to be remembered. These "laws" are arguments in defense of Pressey's _____ _____ program.

(Go to 22-C)

22

A

linear

This program could be visualized as follows, each number representing a frame and the arrow representing the response:

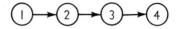

We shall see that great effort is taken to insure that the student will make the correct response. This, again, is a _____ program.

(Go to 23-A)

B

mistakes
errors

According to Skinner, if the student guesses, and guesses incorrectly, he may remember his incorrect guess. Thus, it is important to make the step size so small that the student can always answer correctly. This is one reason that each frame in a linear program consists of a single s_____ s_____.

(Go to 23-B)

C

multiple-choice

The "law of f_____" operates to establish learning when the student is rewarded by making more correct answers than incorrect answers.

(Go to 23-C)

23

A

linear

The nature of the response may be to recognize the correct answer from a selection (multiple-choice) or, as in this case, it may be to **construct** a r_____.

(Go to 24-A)

B

short
step

There is another reason for the short step. The student learns better when he feels successful; correct answers are rewarding to the student. One reason for the short step, then, is to keep the student from making _____ which he may remember.

(Go to 24-B)

C

frequency

Referring to a multiple-choice linear program: "The correct answer is always the last one made" is a function of the "law of r_____."

(Go to 24-C)

24

A

response

     Any question which leaves a blank for you to fill in with a word or phrase (or number) and which does not give you alternatives from which to choose, is said to require a con＿＿＿＿＿＿＿＿＿＿ response.

(Go to 25-A)

B

mistakes
errors

     Another reason for the short step is that, while too many mistakes are discouraging,

c＿＿＿＿＿＿＿ answers are r＿＿＿＿＿ to the student.

(Go to 25-B)

C

recency

     If a student makes more correct than incorrect responses, learning takes place as a function of the "law of f＿＿＿＿＿＿＿."

(Go to 25-C)

25

A

constructed

Give the student strong cues (or hints) at first and then gradually diminish (programmers say "vanish") these cues; and he can answer correctly with less and less help, even when required to **recall** or construct his _____ from memory.

(Go to 26-A)

B

correct
rewarding

To summarize what we've covered so far, the impetus for the type of linear programming exemplified in this chapter stems from the work of _____ _____.

(Go to 26-B)

C

frequency

Pressey's program requires that the student continue to choose from given alternatives until he selects the one correct answer. This factor automatically insures the operation of the "law of _____."

(Go to 26-C)

26

A

response

Any question which leaves a blank to be filled in is said to require a c_____
r_____.

(Go to 27-A)

B

Dr. Skinner

This type of linear programming is characterized by the requirement that the student _____ his _____.

(Go to 27-B)

C

REVIEW

recency

According to Skinner, the _____ _____ is far superior to multiple-choice response.

(Go to 27-C)

A

constructed
response

      Dr. B. F. **Skinner,** through his studies in
behavior, led the way in developing programs
requiring a &rule _____
_____.

(Go to 28-A)

B

construct
responses

      One reason for the constructed response
is the belief that _____ is more efficient than _____.

(Go to 28-B)

C

constructed
response

      Pressey's _____ — _____
program, however, can be given to students
who can't write.

(Go to 28-C)

28

A

constructed
response

Recalling an answer is superior to **rec-
ognizing** an answer in the process of learning
or memorizing, according to Dr. Skinner; and
therefore all his programs require that the
student c＿＿＿＿＿ his ＿＿＿＿＿

(Go to 29-A)

B

recall
recognition

Another reason for constructed responses is the fear that, since learning tends
to take place when the response is made,
presenting likely-sounding alternatives may
cause students to "learn" a(n) ;＿＿＿＿.

(Go to 29-B)

C

multiple-choice

Skinner's insistence on the ＿＿＿＿＿
＿＿＿＿＿ requires machines designed
so that students can write their answers.

(Go to 29-C)

29

A

construct
response

The constructed response, then, which forces the student to recall an answer rather than simply choose from several alternatives, is an identifying feature of the work of Dr. S_____

(Go to 30-A)

B

mistake
error

Also characteristic of this style of programming is the fact that each frame constitutes but one _____ _____ in the total sequence.

(Go to 30-B)

C

constructed
response

In Pressey's program all students eventually must answer each item correctly; thus they all travel the same path. Dr. Pressey's program, therefore, is a _____ program.

(Go to 30-C)

30

A

Skinner

The importance Dr. Skinner attaches to recall is only one reason for his insistence on the _____ _____

(Go to 31-A)

B

short
step

Again, one reason for the short step is to make sure that students will not make _____

(Go to 31-B)

C

linear

Both Dr. _____ and Dr. _____ advocate linear programs.

(Go to 31-C)

A

constructed
response

The very act of **responding** tends to cause **learning,** and giving a student several reasonable-sounding alternatives may cause him to "learn" the wrong one, according to Dr. _____.

(Go to 32-A)

B

mistakes
errors

Another reason for the short step (besides the fear that if a student makes a mistake, he may learn the wrong answer) is that research has shown that students learn better when they are successful. In other words, _____ answers are _____ to the student.

END OF PART I

(Go to 32-B)

C

Pressey
Skinner

Dr. _____'s program can be visualized like this:

①→②→③→④

(Go to 32-C)

32

A

Skinner

There are, then, two reasons for insisting on the constructed response. One is the belief that _____ is more efficient than recognition.

(Go to 33-A)

B

correct
rewarding

Sidney Pressey constructed the first modern teaching machine in 1924. It was based on the multiple-choice principle. In avoiding the multiple-choice style, Dr. S_____ came into direct disagreement with Pressey.

(Go to 33-B)

C

Skinner

Dr. _____'s program can be visualized like this:

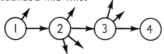

(Go to 33-C)

A

recall

     The other reason for the constructed response (as opposed to recognition responses) is the belief that presenting a student with a choice of alternatives may cause him to learn the wrong answer. This is because the very act of _____ing tends to cause learning.

(Go to 18-B)

B

Skinner

     Dr. Skinner's program can be represented visually like this:

This is a linear program requiring a _____ response.

(Go to 18-C)

C

Pressey

     Both Dr. Skinner's constructed response program and Dr. Pressey's multiple-choice program are _____ programs.

(Go to page 34)

Answer to page 33C: Linear

Now, a summary of Chapter 2:

  I. A linear program is one in which all students read every frame in identical sequence.
 II. One type of linear program is that advocated by Dr. B. F. Skinner, which requires a CONSTRUCTED RESPONSE.
    A. Any question which leaves a blank to be filled in requires a constructed response.
    B. Two reasons are given for preferring the constructed response.
        1. RECALL is more efficient in the learning process than RECOGNITION, according to Skinner.
        2. The act of RESPONDING TENDS TO CAUSE LEARNING; therefore the student should not be exposed to incorrect alternatives.
III. The SHORT STEP is characteristic of all linear programs for two reasons.
    A. If the act of responding tends to cause learning, each step must be short enough so that the student is very likely to answer correctly.
    B. Too many mistakes are discouraging, whereas CORRECT answers are REWARDING to the student.
 IV. The rationale for Dr. Sidney Pressey's multiple-choice linear program is based partly on two factors.

    A. THE LAW OF FREQUENCY: The student may sometimes get a wrong answer, but in each frame he ultimately gets a correct answer. By chance he will get more correct than incorrect answers.
    B. THE LAW OF RECENCY: No matter how many wrong answers a student may try in response to a question, the correct answer is always the last one and is more likely to be remembered because it comes closest to the reinforcement.

CHAPTER 2 — SELF-TEST

The answers may be found on pages 34 and 35.

1. A program in which every student reads every frame in the same sequence is called a _____program.

2. Two men responsible for the development of this style of programming are:

   1_____ 2_____

3. Any question that leaves a blank to be filled in requires a_____   _____.

4. The short step is characteristic of all linear programs for two reasons. What are they?

Please turn the page.

Branching Programming

Examine these "maps."

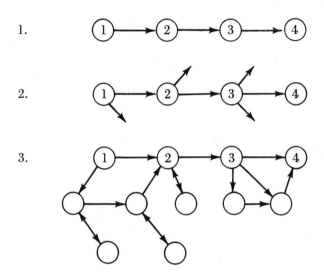

The first two you recognize as linear programs of the constructed response and multiple-choice types respectively. The third represents a new concept, developed by Dr. Norman Crowder. It looks something like the Pressey multiple-choice type, but with a big difference; *the alternatives lead somewhere.*

The branching concept was developed partly on the basis of research in methods of teaching trouble-shooting.
Page 37   What has trouble-shooting to do with branching?
Page 38   Never mind the background — just give me what I need to know about branching.
Page 39   I already know what branching is — but why?

The student of electronics confronted with a piece of faulty equipment may have several equally good places to start looking for trouble; but once he has chosen a starting place, his procedure will differ from that of another student who starts in a different place. Thus, trouble-shooting can be performed in a variety of ways; the object is to teach the student to apply an *effective* procedure without insisting that each student perform in a manner identical to that of every other student. In addition, at many points in trouble-shooting there is no right or wrong answer and it is not desirable to punish the student merely for being different from the instructor.

One alternate training procedure would be to select, arbitrarily, an acceptable path and make all students conform to it; but branching was developed as an attempt to show the student, not that he had made a mistake (or differed from the instructor), but rather what the consequences of his action would be so that he could follow an efficient sequence, always based on the consequences of his last action. Branching, then, permits a variety of attacks on a problem.

Turn to page 38.

Branching, in an elementary form, can be used as a way of explaining why wrong answers are wrong. After each explanation the student can be sent back to the last page to try again:

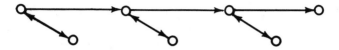

Branching can be used remedially to catch the student who does not understand what has been covered:

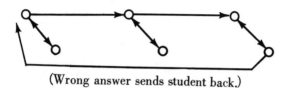

(Wrong answer sends student back.)

Branching can be used to enable the student with a good background to get through faster than the student who needs additional work:

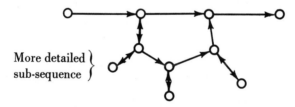

More detailed ⎱
sub-sequence ⎰

Branching can be used to give the student a choice — he can judge how deeply he wants to go, as you did on page 36.

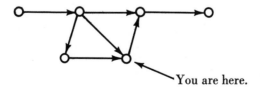

You are here.

Now turn to page 39.

Why branching? Well, as we said earlier, "The alternatives lead somewhere."

Wrong answers, while not encouraged, are not avoided in a branching program as they are in a linear program, since they may be corrected before the learner moves on.

The assumption in branching programming is that a wrong response does not necessarily hinder the learning of a correct response. The *response is useful mainly in guiding the student through the program.* Each response is used to test the success of the latest communication to the student, and in that sense, it "lets the program know" where to take the student next.

The differences in approaches to programming, then, lie in what is considered to be the function of the overt or motor response. The advocates of branching programs believe that:

Page 41   The overt response <u>is not</u> fundamental to the learning process but is useful as a means of supplying feedback to the program.

Page 44   The <u>overt</u> response <u>is</u> fundamental to the learning process.

Page 47   No answer is ever completely wrong.

You asked if I'm saying there are no wrong answers in politics or philosophy.

No, I didn't make myself clear. What I'm saying is that a branching program can ask for facts *or* opinions. The difference is that each opinion branch would proceed on its own prime path (there might be several prime paths running concurrently) while wrong answer branches would ultimately rejoin a prime path.

Please return to page 46 and select another alternative.

Your answer is correct. The overt response, according to Dr. Crowder, is a *measurer* rather than a *fixer* of learning.

Inappropriate responses can be used to uncover misconceptions and areas of weakness and, therefore, have great value.

Since errors or misconceptions are corrected before the learner proceeds, the step size can be larger and the main line (prime path) of the program may proceed more rapidly than in the linear program.

There is always the possibility of having the main-line items proceed in large, fairly difficult steps with shorter, easier stages moving side by side with the main line.

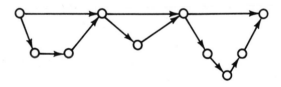

Given a student with the necessary prerequisites, which of the following, in your opinion, would be most dependent on his intelligence?

Page 42   Whether he gets through the program or not
Page 46   How long he takes.
Page 45   How much he knows about the subject upon finishing
          the program

No, there is little correlation between the student's intelligence and his ability to get through a program. The only difference is that bright students go faster.

Please return to page 41 and select another alternative.

You've said you don't understand how politics or philosophy can be branched so that the areas, the depth, and the treatment of the arguments could be tailored to the student.

Suppose a programmer were to set himself the task of showing the student that *whatever his political beliefs are, there is likely to be a convincing argument on the other side.* This would take an astute programmer, but one way he might start would be to ascertain bias:

Which was the better president?

 1. Truman
 2. Eisenhower

With an immediate separation of viewpoints, two prime paths might diverge, never to come together again. Each separate path might treat, in its own way, selected topics. The Marshall Plan, Social Security, foreign and domestic policy might be presented in such a way that, given frequent chances to agree or disagree with principles, the student might maintain a position consistent with his original commitment. He might, however, find himself on the opposite side or, perhaps, somewhere in between.

The point is that correctness of a response is only one of the criteria for branching. We can branch, also, on the basis of learner *opinion*, or on the basis of the probable *consequences* of the learner's responses. Branching can even be based on the proportion of agreement with the response by some population of experts.

Please return to page 46 and select another alternative.

You've got them twisted around. The Skinnerian (constructed-response) programmers believe:

The overt response is fundamental to the learning process — learning takes place when the overt response is made.

The branching programmers believe:

The overt response is best used as a device for evaluation and direction, since learning may have taken place by the time the response is made.

Please return to page 39 and select another alternative.

There seems to be no evidence that a difference in intelligence is reflected in the amount learned from a program.

The assumption is now made that if a student meets the prerequisites and finishes the program, he will score about the same as anybody else on the examination regardless of his I.Q.

> Please return to page 41 and select another alternative.

Right! Given a student with the necessary prerequisites, the only difference intelligence seems to make is in the time it takes to get through the program.

Many questions have more than one possible correct answer, and many questions have no "correct" answer at all but rather express opinion. With a branching program, differing opinions may be given as alternatives, the subject being treated differently, depending on the branch chosen.

This means, for example, that politics or philosophy could be "branched" so that a student's knowledge, ability, and bias could be used to determine the area, the depth, and the arguments used to treat a particular concept.

Page 43 I don't see that at all. Give me an example.

Page 40 Are you saying that there are no wrong answers in politics or philosophy?

Page 48 Opinion branching, it seems, would lead to very long programs.

I just threw this one in to bring you up short if you're getting tired.

But don't be buffaloed into this kind of an opinion — *of course* some things are amenable to right and wrong answers — but not everything that we teach is — and the branching technique allows us to program, for automated instruction, subject matter in which shades of meaning or interpretations are essential.

Please return to page 39 and select another alternative.

Would opinion branching require long programs? Yes, it probably would.

A factual branching program might be very complicated:

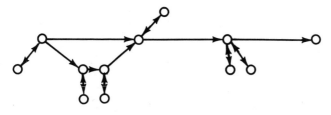

But with opinion branching, several prime paths may run concurrently. Besides that, if a student is asked for an opinion on something he knows nothing about, a sub-sequence may have to be added to teach him the facts. Hence the program might look like this:

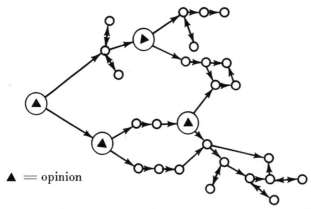

▲ = opinion

The important matter is that the instructional objective is reached, and *this*, rather than length, should be used as the criterion for judging the quality of a program.

Please turn the page.

CHAPTER 3 — SELF-TEST

1. What is the function of the overt response in a branching program? (page 39)
2. Branching items can be based on right or wrong answers. Can you remember any other bases for branching items? (Three more were listed on page 43 but you should remember at least one without looking.)
3. What is the difference between a branching program and the multiple-choice linear program? (page 36)

Please turn the page.

Comparison of Linear

and Branching Styles

Now that you have had some practice with linear and branching program styles, it is appropriate to examine them side-by-side.

Take the matter of feedback. The second criterion of a self-instruction program is that it supplies immediate feedback to the student. In the case of the Skinnerian constructed response program, the evaluation is left up to the student. Suppose the correct answer is "mistakes" and the student answers "errors"; he can decide in that context whether the two words are synonymous. But suppose that the correct answer is $4(x-y)$ and the student answers $4x-y$ — will he notice the difference? Maybe. To what extent, however, should we depend on the judgment of the student?

Page 56   A good programmer will spot these possibilities for error and guard against them with warnings and practice.

Page 53   The problem of almost-correct answers and overlooked mistakes is a problem with constructed-response programs which is not likely to occur with a linear multiple-choice or a branching program.

Wait! Branching has the edge so far, but our arguments aren't all in yet. Some kinds of material are more adaptable to linear programming and there are possibilities for combining the two styles. So please defer your judgment for a little while.

Please return to page 53 and select another alternative.

There is as yet no evidence for this. Students learn well from both linear and branching programs.

It is true, however, that students tend to tire more quickly when working on linear programs. This is not surprising. The pace is slower and more concentrated; there is more repetition; and the student is forced to make more overt responses per unit of time.

Please return to page 63 and select another alternative.

True, the problem of almost-correct answers or overlooked mistakes is not so likely to occur with a branching or multiple-choice linear program, since the student must choose one of the given answers. However, the branching program must anticipate important possibilities for misunderstanding and then provide the opportunity for the student to make the mistake if he does misunderstand. Only in this way can the mistake be corrected.

In the case of the multiple-choice linear program, misconceptions cannot be explained to the student, but possibly making a selection and discovering that it is wrong may cause the student to look twice and find out why.

In programmed *books*, the problem of peeking—or more accurately, of not taking time to formulate an answer before turning the page and looking at the answer—is not as evident in a branching program as it is in a constructed-response program, partly because finding a page in a scrambled book never becomes as automatic as flipping pages in a linear sequence.

Page 59   There is no guarantee that a student will go through any programmed book honestly.

Page 51   Branching seems to have all the advantages.

You answered that branching can't be used in teaching facts, definitions, and skills.

I only offered the suggestion that branching was at its *best* in the area *beyond* facts, definitions, and basic skills, not that branching couldn't handle them. At the same time I suggested that a linear sequence is at its *best* in the area of concept *formation* rather than concept *comparison*.

Please return to page 60 and select another alternative.

You feel that the measure of self-pacing is not reading speed but the freedom to respond rapidly or slowly to the items. I agree, although some don't.

A linear program must cover material with slow, penetrating exactness, building one concept at a time, giving drill where necessary to insure mastery, and then adding concept to concept until a complete picture is formed. It is then tested and rewritten again and again until all "problem" frames are clarified and the student can work through the program successfully. Nothing pertinent to the goal must be taken for granted, since understanding must accompany the student all the way.

Writing a linear program presents an interesting problem. The frame size is small, and the restraint imposed by having to write in short units punctuated by responses and page turnings or machine manipulations makes it difficult to develop a compelling prose style. This, of course, is an individual matter.

Page 63—Did you say that if the student makes a mistake in a linear program, it is the programmer's fault?

Page 62—It seems to me that if all schoolwork were programmed, the student wouldn't ever have the experience of digging something out for himself.

You answered that a good programmer will guard against synonyms or mistakes which might be overlooked.

This can quite possibly be done; but it means, in the case of the synonyms "mistake" and "error," for example, that a reflex must be established to think of a certain *word*. Too often the *concept* slowly sinks out of mind as the word response becomes automatic. By this I mean that the *understanding* that allows the student to substitute an acceptable synonym may be replaced by rote responses in the same way that cliché replaces thought.

In the other case, that of $4(x-y)$ vs. $4x-y$, there are *several* mistakes that could be made either through carelessness or misunderstanding. Are we to belabor every possibility for error — $4x + y$, $(4-x)y$, $4-xy$, etc.—just to guard against the possibility of student inattention?

Although this page is, strictly speaking, a wrong-answer page, I'm glad you turned here. Now, however, please return to page 50 and choose the other answer.

You say it would be easier to teach facts, definitions, and skills with *branching* than to compare concepts and deal with opinion in a *linear* program.

This is probably true, because both branching and linear programs can present a fact and then test for understanding, but only branching programs can, for example, allow the student a choice of opinion and then proceed on the basis of that opinion.

One last point that should be mentioned here: We read some books because we want to master a subject, some simply because we are interested and want to be informed, and some purely for entertainment.

Now, while branching can be every bit as difficult and concentrated as linear programming, it can *also* be used to inform or entertain the interested reader without insisting that he memorize all the details.

The survey, the comparison, the manipulation of concepts— these are naturals for branching, while linear programming works best with the fundamentals, the vocabulary, the building blocks of concepts.

Please turn to page 64.

O.K., I take it back. I wasn't referring to you, anyway. But surely you'll admit that it could happen with a frustrated, unskilled, or lazy teacher.

Please accept my apology, return to page 63, and select another alternative.

No guarantee is possible for any kind of programmed book. The only realistic possibility is to assume that the student will cooperate with the program, just as he "cooperates" with a book, or movie, or instructor. If he doesn't "play fair," he's the loser.

The third criterion for a self-instruction program is that the student works independently with a measure of control over his pace. Linear programming does not have the flexibility in this respect that branching enjoys. A sharp student reading a scrambled book may plow down the prime path and finish the program having actually read fewer than half the pages. A sharp student reading a linear program reads every item that a slow student reads.

Please react to the following criticism of linear programming:

"Because it doesn't meet the third criterion, self pacing, except in terms of reading speed, which doesn't really count, a linear program doesn't actually qualify as a self-instruction program any more than an ordinary textbook does."

Page 61   I accept that statement.

Page 55   The statement is an unjust criticism of linear programming, since the measure of self-pacing is not reading speed but rather the freedom of the individual student to respond rapidly or slowly according to his ability.

Yes, a branching program *is* easier to write than a linear program; but only in the sense that it is easier to make interesting, since the large frame allows the writer to enrich his style, expand his ideas, and introduce correlative material without focusing uniform attention on every item. (The important ideas are brought to the attention of the reader by the response alternatives.) <u>To make a branching program into an instructional tool which meets stated objectives, however, takes as much energy, testing, and rewriting as it takes to make a good program in any other style.</u>

What about the question of appropriate subject matter? Admittedly, this is a very spongy area to try to define. Let me approach it from the edges by suggesting the types of subjects *most easily* handled in linear and in branching programs.

Linear programming is perhaps most appropriate for areas dealing mainly in facts, definitions, and in basic skills which utilize facts and definitions. In mathematics, for example, basic linear sequences can be set up to teach a process; the prerequisites to the goal can be defined, and drilled, and the process evolved, step by step, until a whole concept is developed.

Branching is best used in the area *beyond* facts, definitions, and basic skills. For example, the area of concept *comparison*, such as comparing linear and branching programming, and matters dealing with opinion are better suited to a branching style.

Page 54   In other words, branching can't be used with facts, definitions, and skills.

Page 57   It would be easier to teach facts, definitions, and skills with <u>branching</u> than to compare concepts and deal with opinion in a <u>linear</u> program.

You answered that the linear program cannot be called a self-instruction program since it doesn't allow for self-pacing any more than an ordinary textbook does.

Let's examine this point from two different angles.

When we talked about motion pictures in Chapter I, the point was made that nothing shown to a mass audience could qualify as a "teaching machine" since some students would need time to ponder while some would anticipate answers even before the questions were finished. From *that* point of view the linear program seems to satisfy the criterion.

Now let's look at textbooks. Instead of saying that the linear program is hardly different from a textbook, why not say that the *textbook would be a better self-instruction program if it met the first two criteria?*

If you still feel that linear programs do not meet all three criteria, I'm inclined to say, "Well let's call them self-instruction programs *anyway.*"

Please return to page 59 and select the other alternative.

You indicate that 'the student should have some practice at digging things out for himself.

Quite so. But remember that most teachers spend about 90% of their instructing time at the task of imparting factual information. Now suppose that students could come to class with the facts already in their memories, ready to use. What a fantastic wonderland it would be if the teacher could spend 90% of the time helping students to analyze, synthesize, and evaluate concepts! Imagine the history class in which the students come prepared to discuss the *whys* of history rather than listening to the teacher enumerate the *whats!* Or the algebra class in which—but you get the idea.

(Facts, by the way, are not the only things that can be presented in a self-instruction program—but we'll come back to that point.)

Please return to page 55 and select the other alternative.

If a student makes a mistake, it is the programmer's fault? Exactly. <u>For once in history, the burden of proof is on the teacher (the programmer) and not on the student.</u> At least this is so with linear programming. (The teacher who says of the failing student, "It's all in the book—he's just too lazy to dig it out," might be using that comment as an excuse for poor teaching.)

What about branching in which mistakes may even be welcomed as an opportunity to correct the student who misunderstands without penalizing the student who does understand?

The branching-programmer is under no less obligation to be clear but, as we shall see, the subject-matter most appropriately handled and the way it is approached is different from linear subject-matter. The brancher does not fragmentize the subject into factual bits and lay it out end-to-end. Rather he presents a concept or a cluster of facts as clearly as he can and then answers, on separate pages, whatever important misunderstandings or objections he can anticipate.

Page 60   A branching program is easier to write than a linear program.

Page 52   Students probably learn better from a linear program.

Page 58   I resent that remark you made in parentheses up there in the first paragraph.

CHAPTER 4 — SELF-TEST

Which style of programming would you consider first if you were to program a lesson or book on the following topics?

1. The human skeleton
2. Household budgeting
3. How to clean a fish
4. How to mount a butterfly
5. How to find the square root of a number
6. Methods of psychoanalysis
7. Spelling
8. Should you be in a mental institution?
9. What makes rockets go?
10. Southern Indonesian politics

My opinions are on the next page.

Answer to self-test.

Here is the style I would consider first:

1. *The human skeleton.* It would depend on the purpose. If the purpose were to identify and list the function of the bones, I'd try a linear approach; if it were the formation, the advantages, the restrictions, the nature of bone tissue, etc., I'd try branching first.

2. *Household budgeting.* I would use a branching program, because the rules for budgets vary with income and needs and are not suitable to a restricted linear approach.

3. *How to clean a fish.* An implication of a potentially popular style would lead me to choose branching. Besides, there is more than one way. You might also wish to branch on the basis of different kinds of fish.

4. *How to mount a butterfly.* This suggests a linear approach, since the procedure is fixed and would be memorized.

5. *How to find the square root of a number.* Again, I would try a linear approach for the same reason as 4.

6. *Methods of psychoanalysis.* It would depend again on whether it is a tabulation or a comparative discussion.

7. *Spelling.* Teaching the spelling of words would be easier with a linear program, although the *rules* for spelling could be handled with either style.

8. *Should you be in a mental institution?* One could have a lot of fun with this one—a branching program could consist of situations and a variety of ways of reacting to them, each branch leading closer to a self-imposed diagnosis!

9. *What makes rockets go?* A linear program would serve well to teach the action-reaction law.

10. *Southern Indonesian politics.* This would probably be too spongy for a linear approach.

Please turn the page.

Other Programming Styles

We've talked about only two styles of programs so far. Now let's touch on some of the permutations.

Linear and branching programs may seem to have been treated as if they should forever be kept separate. Even the use of a linear sequence in this book will be recognized as a device to give you an introduction to the style. But is a marriage of the two styles unthinkable?

Why couldn't a linear program be branched at certain checkpoints so that the student who is working well may skip sequences that slower students need? Why couldn't sequences be introduced for the student who needs related background material, and why couldn't ordinary drill sequences be added for the student who demonstrates the need or desire for extra practice?

A linear program could look like this:

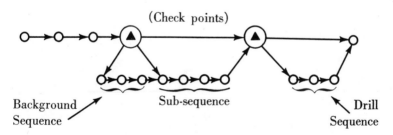

(Check points)

Background Sequence — Sub-sequence — Drill Sequence

Page 73   Wouldn't this technique require a great many extra frames per subject unit?

Page 71   What about introducing <u>linear</u> sequences into a <u>branching</u> format?

Right!

One advantage is that the student will be familiarized with source material. Another is that YOU can teach him how to use these sources, since you can make up the program to suit your local situation. (Although you can use *existing* content materials without having to rewrite it all, do not be misled into believing that it is easier.)

The possibility of injecting into a general science program self-directed field trips to specific locations (a kind of treasure hunt) would certainly focus the student's attention on his environment, and might well serve to spark a latent interest in the subject matter.

Please turn the page.

Another type of program akin to branching is the "self-organizing" program developed by Gordon Pask. This technique, which uses an electronic computer, is extremely useful in teaching motor skills such as the operation of keyboard machines.

For example, in learning to operate an adding machine, the student receives stimuli telling him which buttons to push. As he performs on the keyboard, the computer keeps track of correct responses as well as errors in accuracy, rhythm, touch—anything that is important to learning the operation. As the student improves his skill, the stimuli occur more rapidly; but if a student's ability to strike the proper key improves at the sacrifice of the proper touch, say, the machine senses this and slows down the rate of stimuli, forcing the student to slow down until the particular skill is perfected. As the problem is overcome, the machine again allows the student to speed up. When the student is able to perform a particular exercise at the level established by the programmer, the machine automatically goes on to a more difficult exercise.

The program "branches," but there are an *infinite number* of branching possibilities between perfect response and no response. The computer, constantly sensitive to the performance of the student, is continually modifying or "reorganizing" the program as the student performs.

Page 75 You said keyboard machines—could this include the piano?

Page 69 A piano could probably be hooked into a self-organizing program, but we'd end up with mechanical-sounding pianists.

You shudder at the thought of mechanical-sounding pianists.

The self-organizing program provides a model inside the machine against which the student's performance is scored. The model could be a rendition by the world's greatest pianist and include every nuance of rhythm and dynamics. Admittedly, most piano students don't have the physical ability to copy a difficult piece by a world-famous pianist, but the programmer can adjust the computer to allow a percentage of error. Once the skill is perfected and the student leaves the machine, the performance of the student will accommodate to his own personality, taste, and the regularity with which he practices.

Please return to page 68 and select the other alternative.

Yes, but it's also a good system for those who *can* afford to buy machines.

While your answer is true, your choice of it makes me feel that you don't fully understand. Do not assume that because it can be homemade, it is a poor substitute for a commercial program. On the contrary, because it is tailor-made for a given situation, it may, if it is skillfully done, have far greater strength than a program which has been commercially produced for a mass market.

Please return to page 72 and select another alternative.

What about introducing linear sequences into a branching format? There is no reason this wouldn't work if the material warrants it.

It has been demonstrated that students learn from either style of program and the philosophical differences in rationale, therefore, shouldn't keep programmers from attempting any sort of mixture they need.

Please turn the page.

Another concept of branching programming is called "criterion programming." It is based on the idea that instruction consists of both *content* to be learned and *instructions* to the student and that instructions can be programmed independently of content.

A computer "program," for example, consists of instructions to the computer; the program tells the computer where to get certain numbers, tells it what to do with them, and tells it how to check the accuracy of its operation.

In its application to programming for automated instruction, criterion programming is handled this way:

After it is established that the student meets the prerequisites for successful completion of the program, he is directed to the first content material. He may be instructed to examine a blueprint, or read a paragraph in a book, or look at a motion picture; but whatever the assignment, when he has completed it, he returns to the program, where he is tested. The student's responses to the criterion (test) items are analyzed, and the program, based on this analysis, directs the student to the next content material. He will either be directed to new material or, if his responses indicate the need, he will be directed to corrective or remedial material. Again his performance will be checked and new instructions given. In this way the programmer can use existing materials such as books, pictures, objects, blueprints, films, tapes, locations—anything that is accessible and pertinent to the lesson. Most important, this kind of program can be made by any teacher with a knack for programming and a clear idea of what he wants his students to do.

Page 70 This is a good system for those who can't afford to buy machines.

Page 74 An advantage of this system is that the programming is so much easier to write.

Page 67 An advantage is that the student is indirectly introduced to many sources for the material he is studying.

You feel that the number of frames needed for a branching-linear program would be unduly multiplied.

Look at it the other way. If we build a linear program on the assumption that every step to the formation of a concept must be included to insure that the student understand at every point, then branching provides the student not with something *extra* but with *shortcuts*, when he is able to take them.

Please return to page 66 and select the other alternative.

Sorry!

Anyone who has done any programming will insist that *no* programming is easy.

The task of programming is not so much in writing the program pages as it is in choosing the objectives and organizing the material so that the program can be effectively written.

Please return to page 72 and select the other alternative.

You suggest using a self-organizing program to help students practice the piano.

By all means! This is an excellent potential. The millions of hours spent by piano students in the learning of bad habits and wrong notes stagger the imagination. Connect a self-organizing program to a piano and the student can learn not only the notes but the dynamics, tempo, rhythm, and even pedaling as a total experience under constant supervision.

To the purist who screams that we'll turn out nothing but carbon-copies of Horowitz or Cliburn or Rubinstein I say, what's wrong with sounding like Horowitz, Cliburn, or Rubinstein? Indeed, most piano students would be overjoyed even to produce the musical results of a player piano. The dozen or so that rise to the top each generation will go their own way anyhow, but what a head start they'd have if their practice were always productive!

Alas, we're dreaming. It's merely a mechanical problem but the complexity of a machine that would teach a Beethoven sonata puts the realization of such a program into the future. However, it is now feasible to build machines to teach short exercises and basic note-reading skills. This alone would be a major advance.

Please turn the page.

CHAPTER 5 — SELF-TEST

In this chapter the electronic computer was mentioned in connection with two different types of programming. One type works *like* a computer program, the other actually uses a computer. What name was given to the type of program that works like a computer program? (page 72) What name was given to the type of program that actually uses the computer? (page 68)

2. Referring now to the type of program that is like (but does not actually use) a computer, can you recall some advantages of this type? (Four advantages were listed on page 67.)

3. Is it more feasible to include linear sequences in a branching program than to branch a linear program? (page 71)

Please turn the page.

Conclusion

At last! We have arrived at the stage where we can talk about machines. Much has been said already but a summary of the main types and a short discussion of the kinds of things they can do may help you to evaluate those that are available.

What types are there?

There are constructed response machines in which the student writes his answer on a tape and compares it with the correct answer, which is exposed only when the student's answer is covered with a plastic window (so he can't change it after he sees the correct answer). A variation on this allows the student, after he has written his response, to uncover a clue, (at the same time covering his response with a window). At this point he may write a second response if he wishes to amend the first one. The answer may then be unmasked (at the same time covering the second response with the window), and both answers may then be compared with the correct answer.

There are drill devices in which each item comes back again and again; but when the student answers an item correctly a predetermined number of times, it drops out and does not reappear.

There are constructed response machines in which the student does not write the response but rather constructs his answer mechanically by moving sliders.

There are multiple-choice linear devices which require the student to push buttons, punch holes in paper with a stylus, pull tabs, or type his answer on a keyboard, all of which immediately provide some knowledge of results (i.e., right or wrong).

There is a machine for branching programs which presents the program on a microfilm viewer. The alternatives are selected by a choice of push-buttons.

Finally, there is the computer oriented, self-organizing program for developing motor skills.

What will these machines provide?

First, they all provide an environment in which the learner is, to a greater or lesser degree, in control. *He* decides when "time is up" on a given item, *he* decides when he wants to know the correct

answer. The knowledge that his mistakes will be recorded makes the control meaningful and motivates him to attend to the problem. From the teacher's point of view, the recording of responses permits evaluating both the effectiveness of the program and the performance of the individual student. Based on this record, the teacher may provide guidance or assistance as needed.

Second, because the machine is to a greater or lesser degree responsive to the student, it provides an environment in which outside distractions are less noticeable. The student whose mind wanders during a lecture may miss an important point; a machine will not proceed unless the student is ready. The more attractive the learning situation, the more readily will students apply themselves to it. Motivational devices such as visible counters and timers, lights, and even buzzers are available on some machines.

Third, although the initial cost of a branching machine is high, the program is stored on microfilm and thus is less costly and requires far less storage space than the equivalent program in scrambled book form.

Fourth, machines may add a dimension of interaction that could not be achieved in any other way. The self-organizing program represents a constant and highly sensitive interaction between student and machine in the learning of motor skills; designs are feasible that would allow similar treatment of verbal subject matter. A computer with an undistractable brain ready instantly to call forth any information in its memory bank could, on the basis of student response to test items, redirect the student to any number of alternate paths, depending on the background and even the temperament of the student. Because a computer could time responses and compare them with all other responses, it could allow the student to compete with his own past performance, with his aspirations, or with other students. The machine could decide, on the basis of the time taken for each response, whether the student needs simpler steps or harder steps. It could, by constant testing, *prevent* the student from stumbling through the program without really paying attention. These designs are still speculative, however, and will require considerable research and improvement in programming techniques and skills before they can be realized.

How do we decide what kind of presentation device to buy?

First, decide what you want to teach and write out your teaching objectives in *behavorial* terms. That is, state your desired outcomes in terms of measurable behavior ("to be able, in ten minutes or less, to extract the square root of a three-digit number, using only pencil and paper") and avoid unmeasurable objectives ("to understand how square root is extracted").

Second, examine any available programs to see if they meet your stated instructional objectives.

Third, decide how much control is desirable in the self-instructional situation.

Fourth, examine as many different program holders and machines as you can. If an expensive machine doesn't satisfy any more of your requirements than a simple program holder, then consider the inexpensive program holder. But remember that cost alone is a false factor; if the machine you need happens to be expensive, you will only waste money buying anything else.

Now, one last branch:

Page 80   Self-instruction programs may be used not only for present factual information but may be used to help the student develop positive attitudes toward a subject.

Page 81   Self-instruction programs are fine for studying facts but the task of guiding the student's attitude formation must be left to the real live teacher.

Right you are!

Books have been doing this for centuries—even textbooks.
What is a teacher for?

A teacher is a self-organizing program with infinite possibilities for guiding and interacting, transmitting attitudes, re-directing or orienting the student. The fewer machine jobs the teacher has to do, the more time will be available for the student to exploit and benefit from this human skill. After all, it has been said that any teacher who can be replaced by a machine, probably ought to be!

CHAPTER 6 — SELF-TEST

What four steps must be taken before selecting any presentation device?

This is the end of the program.

You don't really believe that, do you?

Have you never been excited over something that you've read? Doesn't a good textbook present the facts *and* inspire an attitude? *Remember*, a good program is built by a good teacher.

Please return to page 79 and select the other alternative.

82

A Brief Bibliography

This short list is designed to direct you to the source materials, the bibliographies, and some of the periodicals that are devoted in full or in part to programmed instruction.

Source books:

Fry, Edward B., Glenn L. Bryan and Joseph W. Rigney. "Teaching Machines: An Annotated Bibliography," *A-V Communication Review,* Vol. 8, Supplement 1, 1960. Washington, D.C., Department of Audiovisual Instruction, National Education Association. 80p.

Galanter, Eugene, ed. *Automatic Teaching: The State of the Art.* New York, John Wiley and Sons, 1959. 198p.

Lumsdaine, Arthur A. and Robert Glaser. *Teaching Machines and Programmed Learning; A Source Book.* Washington, D.C., Department of Audiovisual Instruction, National Education Association, 1960. 724p. Extensive bibliography.

Periodicals devoted entirely to programmed instruction:

AID; Auto-Instructional Devices for Education and Training. Lubbock, Texas, Institute of International Research and Development.

Automated Teaching Bulletin. Los Angeles, Rheem Califone Corporation.

Programed Instruction. New York, The Center for Programed Instruction.

Periodicals which include articles or sections on programmed instruction:

Audiovisual Instruction. Washington, D.C., Department of Audiovisual Instruction, National Education Association.

Lumsdaine, Arthur A., ed. "Instructional Media," *Contemporary Psychology.* Washington, D.C., American Psychological Association.

Lumsdaine, Arthur A., ed. "Teaching Machines and Auto-Instructional Programs," *A-V Communication Review.* Washington, D.C. Department of Audiovisual Instruction, National Education Association.

Slide-a-Mask, Dyna-Slide Co., Chicago

Vertimask, Dyna-Slide Co., Chicago

Atronic Portable Tag, General Atronics Corporation, Bala Cynwyd, Pa.

The Atronic Tag in use

*Autoscore, Astra Corporation,
New London, Conn.*

*Multiple-Choice Machine,
Rheem-Califone Corporation,
Hollywood, Calif.*

*TM-3 Discoverer,
Billerett Company,
Anaheim, Calif.*

*Didak 501, Rheem-
Califone Corporation,
Hollywood, Calif.*

*Min/Max, Teaching Materials
Corporation, New York City.*

*Foringer 2002,
Programmed Teaching
Aids Inc., Arlington, Va.*

*Ferster Tutor, Programmed
Teaching Aids Inc.,
Arlington, Va.*

*Koncept-o-Graph,
Teaching Machines
and Program
Developers,
Rochester, N. Y.*

Atronic Tutor, General Atronics Corporation, Bala Cynwyd, Pa.

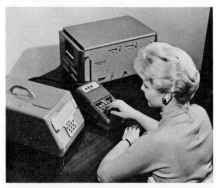

Solartron, Rheem-Califone Corporation, Hollywood, Calif.

Mark II Autotutor, Western Design and Electronics, Goleta, Calif.

Mark I Autotutor, Western Design and Electronics, Goleta, Calif.